How a locked exit gave me a way out

ROB GODDARD

First published in 2016
This 2nd edition published in 2019

Published by Rob Goddard Books
www.robgoddard.co.uk
rob.goddard@robgoddard.co.uk

ISBN: 978-1-9162204-0-9 (paperback)
ISBN: 978-1-9162204-1-6 (ebook)

I dedicate this book to my six children, Tom, Josh, Haydn, Phoenix, Lizzie and Katie. Without you, life would lack the meaning that it does. I'm not the "perfect" Dad, but I love each of you so very much. I'm very proud of you all.

And to Kristina ... we have been the best of friends for so many years and now we are life partners together. You keep me grounded and supported. Life with you is a wonderful exploration and above all else, tremendous fun.

With much love

EARLY REVIEWS

"Winning at sport and winning in business have many cross-overs. Preparation, persistence and the desire to be the best in your chosen field are all fundamental to performance excellence. Rob's books are designed to help increase the potential and value within all of us."

Roger Black MBE and Steve Backley OBE, Olympic Medal Winners

"Congrats Rob! I could see and feel that you'd make a huge impact with your story. Sharing your heart will transform them much more than business"

Dr Andrea Pennington, International Speaker and CEO of Make Your Mark Global

"Impressive!"

James Caan CBE, Investor and formerly of Dragons' Den

CONTENTS

All profits from this book go to CALM
(Campaign Against Living Miserably)

CALM is leading a movement against male suicide, the single biggest killer of men under 45 in the UK.

www.thecalmzone.net

0800 58 58 58

OUR MISSION

If this book has found its way into your hands, please read it. The chances are that it was handed to you by somebody who wants to be your 'Alex' – the person you know you can talk to about the way you're feeling.

When you've finished it and you're feeling stronger, observe more closely the male friends, acquaintances and colleagues you see regularly or sporadically. Are any of them secretly hiding similar feelings to your earlier low moods? Do they need you to be their own 'Alex'?

Perhaps it's time to start a conversation with them. You can do it very simply by passing them this book.

Sign your name in solidarity with other people who have suffered depression and anxiety over the page and state the city in which you read this book. As the next reader sees who has 'owned' the book before, he'll gain confidence from your visible support. Then, go to www.robgoddard.co.uk and let us know that you've signed the book so that we can add you to our family of expressive, supportive men. You can also leave a message for future readers at the back of this book.

If you are the fiftieth person to sign here (the last numbered line), please post the book to:

Merlin House, Brunel Road, Theale,
Berks RG7 4AB United Kingdom

That will enable us to see how far the book has travelled and just how the good news about depression and anxiety is spreading around the world.

1.
2.
3.
4.
5.
6.
7.
8.
9.
10.
11.
12.
13.
14.
15.
16.
17.
18.
19.
20.
21.

22.
23.
24.
25.
26.
27.
28.
29.
30.
31.
32.
33.
34.
35.
36.
37.
38.
39.
40.
41.
42.
43.
44.
45.
46.
47.
48.
49.
50.

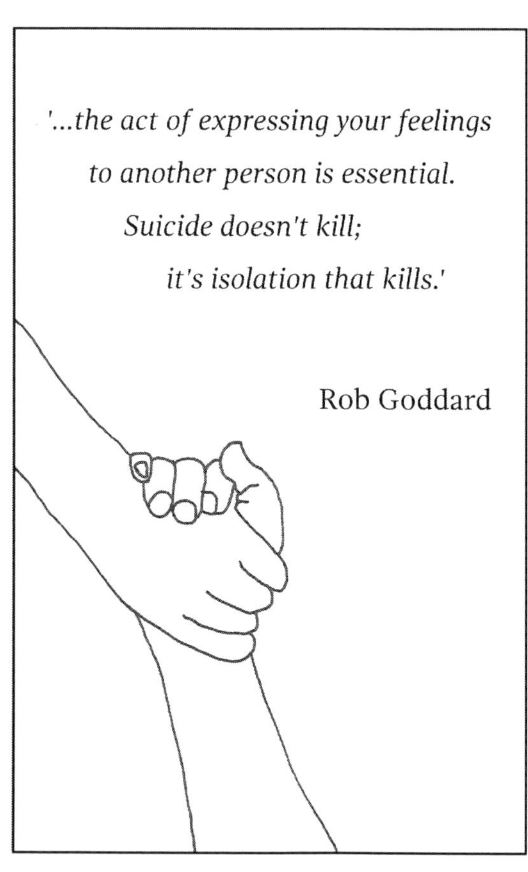
'...the act of expressing your feelings
to another person is essential.
Suicide doesn't kill;
it's isolation that kills.'
Rob Goddard

FOREWORD

This is not intended as a 'business book'. While it touches on several entrepreneurial themes that you can read about at length elsewhere, this book touches on one which very rarely gets mentioned.

The fact is that entrepreneurship and depression frequently walk hand in hand. When it's left unaddressed, depression and anxiety often lead to thoughts of suicide – now recognised as the leading cause of death in men under fifty years old.

I was very nearly one of them.

This is my story. I'm sharing it with you as I learned from my good friend, Alex Petty, that recovery starts when you share what you're thinking and feeling. With his help, I began my path to wellness. Thank goodness for Alex.

The world needs more 'Alexes'.

Don't hesitate to reach out for support if you're dealing with depression. There's far more awareness these days of how depression can affect someone and more 'Alexes' around than ever. Far from 'keeping it quiet', men of all ages are opening up - talking about it, giving and receiving help.

HOW TO FIND YOUR 'ALEX'

For many men, starting a conversation about depression feels difficult. Yet it's when you start to talk about it with someone you trust that your recovery may begin. There's been such a stigma attached to depression in the past that it's easy to forget that it's a real health condition. You can't expect to overcome it without help.

Talking about it does not make you weak, a burden or 'crazy'.

You know how good it feels to be able to help someone ... accept a little support now and one day, you'll have your turn to pass the favour on.

Look around your close and extended circle of contacts. Who could you speak to about how you're feeling and thinking?

A friend, your partner or family member?

A therapist or coach?

Your GP, or someone who understands depression?

A faith leader?

Someone you like and trust at work?

HOW TO BE AN 'ALEX' FOR SOMEONE ELSE

Is there somebody you know who might be struggling with depression or anxiety? It can be difficult knowing what to say to them that might help them.

Actually, it's simpler than you think.

- » Put real time aside to listen closely to them
- » Avoid alcohol while you're together – it can make things a lot worse for them
- » Don't offer advice; just listen, face-to-face
- » Encourage them to carry on speaking, saying things like "Thank you for telling me this", or "Go on – tell me why you think that."

Remember, you don't have to agree with their point of view. You just need to listen to it.

If they say that they have had thoughts about suicide, take it seriously. They may need urgent help and you should contact a helpline or your local Mental Health Services right away on their behalf. If you feel that they might be in danger of self-harm, stay with them until you have support.

Finally, thank you for stepping up and being an 'Alex'. The world needs more supportive people like you!

Burj Khalifa – It's a very long way down

PROLOGUE

2012

I'm making my way to the upper floors of Burj Khalifa, Dubai – the tallest building in the world. That's probably why it has the longest elevator journey of any building in the world – even if it is one of the fastest. Just one minute to climb one hundred and twenty-four floors to the first observatory deck. Right now, I'm in it. Roughly halfway up and I'm training my thoughts on trivia.

It's not the only world record this building holds. Up here, 2717 feet above the ground, there's the world's highest nightclub and the world's highest restaurant, not to mention the world's highest New Year fireworks display.

My elevator companions step out from the dark interior of the elevator onto the floor of the observatory and I wince from the sudden impact of light. Dazzling, shocking light everywhere – pouring through glass walls from floor to ceiling. A few sightseers amble about, dazed and disorientated, slackly holding mobile phones in front of their chests, unable to decide what to photograph first.

I'm treated to an inviting view of the world far, far below us, so distant that I can follow the curve of the horizon. The world is already smaller from up here. Less consuming.

As I finally step out of the elevator half a mile up in the air, I find someone to take a couple of last photographs of me on my phone. I have to find a fire exit that leads to Floor 163 - the exclusive stomping ground of the building mechanics, just at the base of the spire.

Even here, everywhere shimmers. In my mind's eye, the view from the surrounding wall of windows rocks me and I reflexively shoot out a hand to steady myself. There's nothing to hold onto, of course. The architects have taken care not to spoil anybody's clear view with bars, ledges or openings of any kind.

Except for one. The Fire Exit door stands shut to my right.

The shot of adrenaline makes me gasp and step forwards, reaching for the lever. With both hands, I grasp it and jerk it downwards.

It's locked. Who the hell locks a Fire Exit?

CHAPTER ONE

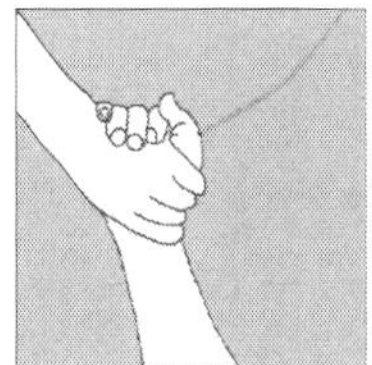

Life in a commune

1998

The good folks of our community church in Chino, Los Angeles welcomed us warmly and our twin boys, Tom and Josh, took to the communal family thing like ducklings to water. They were only two years old at the time, so they knew nothing of the change of life and upheaval that Sharon and I had made. It was one big nursery school for them. As they scampered about with thirty other children, they did so under the watchful eyes of about sixty adults. The expression "it takes a village to raise a child" might have been invented there. They became "Community Kids", looked after and loved by the others in our group.

For me, the Christian Food Ministry was a real "boot camp" experience. I had just left a well-paid job in the UK at a bank and was all set to become Bank Manager - a position regarded in the early Eighties as one of the three pillars of a business community, along with its lawyers and accountants.

That would have pleased my mum, but I grew restless and disillusioned with the sector. It seemed far too restrictive and rule-driven for me. Free expression, initiative, and spontaneity weren't high on the list of corporate priorities for an established, high street Bank: it was more about maintaining the status quo and ensuring conformity. Life became tedious and devoid of challenge. It was time for a change ... time to take my first big leap into the unknown.

So here we were in a new country, feeding seven to eight hundred hungry, homeless and poor Hispanic people alongside our new brothers and sisters in the little church. As Christians, we'd felt that this type of work was a part of our spiritual calling.

Chino is not on the tourist trail. It's primarily known for two things: cows and a state penitentiary. It hardly compares to the glitzy world of Los Angeles - "La La Land" as it's affectionately called. It's where Sharon's cousins led a small, dynamic church and it made sense to us to be there, living with a sense of purpose as we served our new community. It was the kind of 'on the edge' Christianity that had immense appeal, especially for me. We were set for some hard work, living in a neighbourhood with drive-by shootings and wide-spread poverty.

It couldn't have been further removed from the restrictive, buttoned-up, UK banking industry. This was Life in its raw state; we were truly making a difference to others and I felt switched on, awake and filled with energy. Feeding, supporting and being friends with many forgotten and unwanted local people was a very humbling experience. Together with our team, Sharon and I would venture into many local communities with a truck loaded with tons of food, bagging it up and handing it out on the streets with the rule that we gave each person as much as they could carry.

Christmas especially was an extravaganza. People donated over twenty thousand toys which we sorted into gender and age groups. We ended up renting an old Bank of America building for a dollar a month so that we could store and distribute all of these gifts. At last! A bank that was committed to giving rather than taking!

People gave generously because they could see the proof of the change we were trying to affect in the community. The outreach was respected, with very little sense of a "them and us" attitude. To be fair, Sharon and I were living almost as basically as the people we were serving in the communities. At the time, we were given just ten dollars a week plus free food and accommodation.

I supplemented this with some landscaping and gardening maintenance work at the homes of L.A.'s middle classes with some other guys. What did I know about gardening? Absolutely nothing, but I lost several stones in weight working in temperatures of thirty-five degrees or more! I still love gardening to this day.

*

There's a group of about thirty people in front of us, some chatting with each other and others standing still, staring at us and waiting for the entertainment to start. The headline act hasn't arrived yet, so we're doing our best to warm up the crowd and keep them here.

Tim is really wired. In between every song he fiddles with his acoustic, tuning and retuning, looking up and down the street. Word's out that none other than Glen Matlock of "The Sex Pistols" fame is joining us tonight with his guitar. Imagine that! Our little outreach group has stirred up such a great response around here that we're getting celebrity backing now!

A group of three prostitutes hangs out on the corner opposite, with another one slowly walking along the kerb several metres away from them. Apart from a brief nod in our direction when we arrived and started singing, they've ignored us all evening. Now though, they're looking nervous, pulling handbags up higher on their shoulders and putting out cigarettes with their stilettos.

The reason is clear. Down the street from around the corner, a gang of at least a dozen youths swaggers into view. They're heading towards us, smirking and silent, walking as a pack behind their leader.

The working girls walk away, as slowly as their fear will allow them. This is not a place to hang out for kicks. This is one of the most dangerous streets in the world. Skid Row, downtown Los Angeles, internationally infamous for its drug trade, knife crime and pimping.

Just perfect for a singalong, then.

I swallow hard and pray. I guess if we're going to get a kicking, then at least we'll get it altogether. We've become something of a family, facing everything and supporting each other with a deep commitment. We're on a mission, after all; there's nothing more binding and blessed than a common cause for good.

Tim strikes up the chorus of "Together We Are Love". It's as inappropriate as "If You're Happy and You Know It", but it's too late now. They've reached us. They're splitting up and moving menacingly around the onlookers who wish they'd never fallen for the Glen Matlock story and stayed away tonight.

My heart pounds. The seconds tick by ... Tim misses a down strum as we all draw a little closer together, grinning like maniacs in a vain attempt to appear calm to our trapped audience. What do these guys want? They're just standing there, with their backs to us, positioned between the crowd and the rest of the street.

Tim catches my eye and grins. Then it dawns on me: these guys aren't here to cause trouble. They're here to protect us. Seriously, our outreach has gained even the respect of the gangland.

Amazed, I shake my head as Tim laughs at my face. He has more to be happy about, as a black leather-clad, skinny bloke emerges from a car a few metres away with his guitar.

A long, loud cheer arises from the crowd and Tim leads us in song with more gusto than before to give Glen Matlock the welcome he deserves.

Tonight's going to be great. So many highs. A mission that's drawn a whole community together. A gig to remember with the best family in the world.

Pity it's not actually Glen Matlock, but I'd never tell Tim that. That's what mates are for.

*

We worked hard and learned how to live on very little for eight months in Chino. As with so many things that start off well, though, the mission work slowly became tainted for us. What had started out as a small church became more of a cult, with the leaders controlling their little flock with no accountability to anyone else.

What they said went; misappropriation of donated money, heavy-handed authoritarianism, psychological abuse through accusation and isolation – and there was no escaping it easily.

Several people tried in the dead of night but were discovered and brought back to the commune, shamed and humiliated.

It's hard to halt disillusionment once it starts to grow, especially if the issue isn't resolved. Sharon and I were asking the same, searching questions as before. Without jobs to go to, or even a home, we headed back to the UK. We had little to our names as we had sold up everything to work overseas in the first place.

Nothing in life is ever wasted, though. We both still had a longing to make a difference in life. My lifestyle experience at the outreach prepared me for what was to come, although I didn't know it at the time. If commercial life in banking had hardened my heart towards people and made me selfish, my time in Chino had softened it once more.

CHAPTER TWO

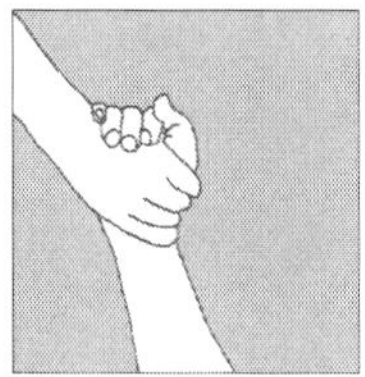

Starting over again

Miraculously, within weeks of our returning from Los Angeles, we found a home and I found a job. We had the love and support of our home church in the UK, too, which was instrumental in us integrating back into "normal" life.

However, we didn't want normal life. We'd spent eight months living on the edge, achieving something that fulfilled us. The idea of slipping back into a life of normal, everyday mundanity was anathema. We wanted to use our experience of living for every moment - mindful, useful and spirit-full - as a springboard for our lifestyle back in the UK.

That was easier said than done.

I landed a job on thirteen thousand pounds a year plus bonuses. Granted, it was significantly more than ten dollars a week back in Chino, but it was a telesales job and I really hated the thought of cold calling. I've always avoided such work, but it was that or nothing, so I threw myself into it. We had the "normal" things to look after, of course - rent, other bills to pay and two young children to feed.

I spent four years in the company and in that time became Head of Operations. While I was there, I discovered that I really liked being part of a small privately-owned company. I knew life in the corporate world wasn't for me anymore. Being involved in a more flexible and fast-growing environment was much more exciting and satisfying.

I was involved in helping to raise twenty million dollars from private equity for the UK business to set up in the States. I was firmly back in the world of business, but this time working for a rapidly growing small to medium-sized enterprise (SME).

I liked the nature of an SME. You can make a notable difference without too much red tape and bureaucracy in a smaller business. I found it easier to demonstrate my personal contribution to the overall growth of the company than I had in corporate banking. There, you're a very small cog in a huge wheel; you get lost in the 'machinery teeth' of a bank.

There's something about a brief moment of contentment in business that encourages goal setting. I believe in goals. They allow you to attach an emotional outcome to your hard work – to really feel excited about what you're doing, where you're going. So, with my newfound joie de vivre, I wrote them down:

GOALS!
Retire at 55 years old
Move to Greece
Teach English to Greek kids

Why Greece? Well, I was looking for somewhere warm, with a slower pace of life. It also needed to be close enough to fly back to the UK to visit the family.

Why teaching? I saw it as a passport to working in another country. Yes, the wanderlust was nibbling at me again.

I studied and qualified as a teacher under the TEFL scheme ("Teaching English as a Foreign Language") and taught a part-time evening class for two years at a local college to practice my newfound skills. I loved it!

It wasn't so much the teaching of a language that I enjoyed; it was more the interaction with other people. We shared things about British life and culture, which was most rewarding. Also, it was learning about other cultures in the classroom: Polish, Czech, Albanian, Romanian, Chinese and Japanese. I encouraged my students to share information about their own country and customs, too.

It was in that same year that I was approached by another privately-owned company, a well-established Mergers and Acquisitions firm, that had plans for significant growth. They asked me to join as General Manager to help deliver that growth, which I did: a tenfold increase in sales within seven years, as it turned out.

It was a fantastic experience which brought out qualities and skills that I didn't know I had. I found that I could make things happen and make money, not only for myself but for other people - shareholders, staff and clients.

At last I had found a career that suited me to the ground!

How had this happened? I was positively demonstrating characteristics of a real-life entrepreneur. When had I become one of those?

I suppose I developed a range of skills when I was in banking but I was totally unaware of them at the time. Yes, I was good at selling, but this was different. Working in a small but growing business was more about having a vision, organising resources and making it happen. It was also about having a "nose" for good business and generating attractive profits from sometimes limited resources.

For the second time in my life, I tasted fulfilment. As business success grew, so did my personal income. I ended up in the top 1% of earners in the country.

The commune days in Chino spent feeding the poor slipped further away ... I gained in self-confidence, self-importance and sales speak. I began to believe my own hype and to forget what I'd learned there: that material things and good fortune can be stripped from you in an instant.

They were about to be stripped from me, too.

CHAPTER THREE

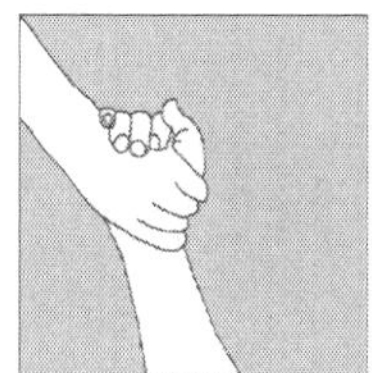

The collapse of my world

During the second half of 2008, I lost my job, my home and my marriage.

All down to me; no-one else's fault but mine. It was an earth-shattering moment in my life that rocked the very foundation of my world.

The life I had taken decades to build and nurture was blown away in a matter of a few months and worse still, by my own stupid actions. This is not the book to go into detail of what occurred, but suffice to say, I lost sight of what was important in my life at that time.

Our lives can be very fragile. Often, we think they're robust and built on rock. More often than not, it's more like they're built on shifting sands.

In fewer than ten years, I had changed from feeding the poor as a missionary to an ego-centric businessman. I'm not entirely sure how that transition happened but happen it did.

The pursuit of career and money became intoxicating and exciting for me. It was like a drug. I was walking into shops without bothering to find out the price of anything. I bought a series of brand new Harley Davidsons and luxury cars. On one cruise I bought a dozen original paintings on board the ship at an auction. The bill, slipped under the cabin door the night before disembarkation, was eye-watering, even for me! Money had very little value because I had so much of it.

The trouble is also that we can often surround ourselves with "things" to make us happy and content. Symbols that life is good to us and that we are successful. This is, in fact, an illusion.

Happiness, contentment and true success come from somewhere else - somewhere deep down from within you. An inner knowledge that you're at peace with who you are and can enjoy being in the "moment."

The Eastern religions understand something about this:

"If you love someone, the greatest gift you can give them is your presence. If you love someone but rarely make yourself available to him or her, that is not true love. The most precious gift we can offer anyone is our attention. When mindfulness embraces those we love, they will bloom like flowers." (Thich Nhat Hanh)

You can't buy happiness and contentment; you can only experience it.

My life in 2008 was far from this utopian existence. I became jobless, ending up with creditors of huge debts circling like vultures. What's even worse, I'd separated from my wife, leaving her behind living at home with my two sons.

How can I express the pain of the separation from my children? It was the thought of the pain I inflicted on them that was the most difficult to bear because they were not at fault; they had become victims in a situation that I created.

To this day, I still carry that guilt with me. Your dad is supposed to be infallible when you're little; sadly, my sons discovered that theirs was not.

No family, no job, no savings and no self-esteem ... I began to sink into an ever lengthening, downward spiral emotionally and psychologically.

Loneliness and isolation became part of my condition, as did extreme anxiety and panic about the future. Being in the state of mind that life is not worth living and the world doesn't really care is a very scary place. It becomes a vicious cycle and wasn't helped by me renting single rooms on a short-term basis.

Perhaps it was time to see a doctor.

*

"Come in, Rob," she smiles, backlit by brilliant sunshine in the doorway. It feels like I'm walking towards the proverbial 'white light' of the afterlife.

I look down at the form and its list of questions. The usual sort of thing – date of birth, occupation, marital status, past physical health problems, current physical health problems, blah blah. She must have most of this on record in any case.

I work my way through them one by one.

"Do you stress over trivial problems?" Probably – but who's to say they're trivial?

"Do you find it difficult to relax?" Oh, please ... I can't remember the last time I was relaxed. A hollow laugh escapes me and the doctor catches my eye. She's perfectly serious about this questionnaire.

Bloody red tape.

Shifting in my chair I resolve to behave myself and submit to the useless official process – just get it over with and get out of here.

"Have you had, or do you have, thoughts of suicide or harming yourself?"

Wait – what? I read it again.

"Have you had, or do you have, thoughts of suicide or harming yourself?"

The print seems to leap out of the page towards me. That word ... it rings loudly inside my head as I read it, gazing at it for what seems an age. There's a twisting in my stomach, my palms are suddenly clammy and cold. I can feel the blood drain from my face as the room starts to spin. Everything in it seems further away – smaller, insignificant.

Nothing matters at all. For how long has nothing mattered at all?

I steady myself and reach for some water. In a moment of searing clarity, I need to make a decision. Which way do I want to go?

I opt for the truth and pick up the pen.

"Yes."

*

At that moment, my eyes immediately welled up with tears. I felt an immense surge of uncontrollable emotion like a dam finally breaking. I admitted to myself that I had a serious problem – one that I couldn't control. I tried to describe how I was feeling to the doctor but had to fight hard to utter words in coherent sentences.

My declaration in writing that I was prepared to end my life and disappear from the world made it real to me that I was suffering from severe depression. I hadn't admitted it to myself until that point. I had always viewed people with depression as "weak-minded." Now, I was experiencing it for myself and yet I knew that I wasn't weak-minded.

Was this really how it felt for others that I'd known to be depressed? Were others going to judge me the same way, now?

I was prescribed a collection of drugs and referred to counselling. I recall reading the notes they always insert in the boxes of tablets and being rather bemused by the statement that one of the side effects of taking these anti-depressants was that it might cause depression!

I wasn't eating properly. Instead, I consumed alcohol to "self-medicate" when my body started to get used to the effects of the prescribed drugs. It was a spiral I felt I couldn't break. The unbearable, repetitive patterns of thinking and emotional pain that hurt with an almost physical twisting in my stomach had to stop. I turned to the internet to look up ways of killing myself, ideally without any pain.

There is an astounding number of articles out there on suicide. I pored over them, moving from one to the next as soon as I reached the grim bits. I came to the conclusion that there was no guaranteed way of dying without pain, which was disappointing.

One post struck me, though. It stood out from the rest and while it might have appeared trite at the time, I just couldn't get it out of my mind later. It said:

"Suicide is a long-term solution to a short-term problem."

I think that it sank into my subconscious somehow.

The depression was a dark ominous cloud that invaded my world whenever it chose, enveloping my space and my thoughts. The array of medicines helped, eventually, to stabilise my condition but in three years of my taking them they never rid me of depression.

*

After some time of my taking the medication, I started to see a close friend, Lisa, romantically.

I can't say that I was in the best condition to start a relationship. However, I moved in with her and she did her best to support and encourage me. It was extremely hard for her, though; I was damaged goods, both mentally and emotionally. My life was centred on the wrong priorities: I was desperately trying to build something stable on shifting sands instead of rock. Despite that, we have two lovely daughters – a loving testament to our time together.

With Lisa's help, I developed some basic routines that weren't too onerous and which managed to stop me from dwelling on my depression, even if just for a short while. Daytime television helped me to forget just how lousy my life really was; there was always someone on "The Jeremy Kyle Show" in those days who had it worse than I. "Come Dine With Me" with David Lamb's tongue-in-cheek sense of humour was better at lifting my spirits and fanned an old flame for cooking back into life. It was a good escape for an hour a day from the depressing world I inhabited.

However, I wasn't bouncing back to my normal self; it was just existence, not true living. As the months ticked by, I was not improving.

Lisa encouraged me to see a psychotherapist. The combined cognitive behavioural therapy (CBT) and hypnotherapy helped me to a degree, as did the opportunity to talk each week with a complete stranger about my overwhelming problems.

I learned the technique of visualising myself in a plastic sphere protected from what was outside, contained in my own bubble; from inside, I could see and hear what was going on outside but somehow it didn't affect me. This made me feel empowered. I began to see that my own space around me needn't be affected by Life and its stresses. It was my private space, unaffected by others.

Finally, I felt as though I had some degree of control back in my life. I could build on this, I thought.

CHAPTER FOUR

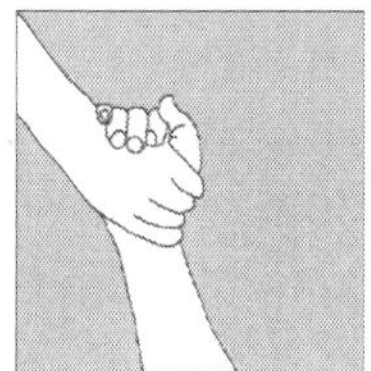

Rebuilding

It was also at this time I set up my own business, offering business consultancy and advice. After all, no-one was going to employ me in this state! I really didn't want to work for myself but I had no choice; the employment market was pretty much dead and I had some chunky bills to pay.

I started my new business from my bedroom with a broadband connection, a basic website and some business cards. Then, I networked like hell. No-one knew I existed, what I offered and how I might be able to help them.

I felt a fraud, though. I had no business, really. I was just starting out on my own and I was contemplating suicide virtually every day. I can even remember breaking down into tears as I was driving to one networking event in Newbury. Uncontrollable tears about what Life had become for me and how there was no hope left.

*

As I switch off the engine and the radio goes quiet, I'm left listening to the rain on my windshield and my own gaspy breathing. Giving my eyes a couple of minutes to change from bloodshot to merely haunted, I blow my nose and straighten my tie. This is a networking meeting, Rob – get a grip, I tell myself. You can go off and have a good blub afterwards – not now, though.

I step out into the rain and head for the door. A couple of smiling suits welcome me and show me into a room buzzing with sales pitches. They're all the same, these networking groups. Just for once, it would be refreshing to come to one and actually meet someone who wasn't trying to get you to buy something. Someone who actually spoke sense and you just instinctively knew was a good type. Someone who –

"Hi! It's Rob, right?"

A guy with a grin and a laid-back air appears at my elbow.

"Alex Petty. Glad you came here. It's a good place. What can I do to help you grow your business?"

What can he ...? No-one's ever asked me that. I'm stunned. He's not trying to sell me anything. He's focused on me, not himself. That's novel.

I look him up and down. Looking straight into his eyes is a bit unnerving. It's like he knows I'm on the brink of tears again.

"I've just started out on my own, actually ..." I stutter. My coffee sloshes a bit into its saucer. "I guess I'm looking for new business leads."

The guy nods brightly. "How many do you need?"

What's with him? That's two great questions in a row and I don't have ready answers. Best to put him off – get him out of my face. He'll lose interest when he hears I'm a useless prospect.

"I haven't a clue. I don't even have a strategy, a plan, a financial forecast or even a budget, to be honest."

"Oh, right," he says, handing me his cup and reaching for his business card. "Well, then – let's get together."

*

Although I didn't know it at the time, Alex was to become my rock – one of the most important people in my life. He was part of a national business coaching group and introduced me to their fantastic ninety-day planning events – just what I needed then.

They gave me focus, tactics and strategy for the next three months ahead. At the same time, Alex offered wise counsel on things from the sidelines. I learnt that to set up in business you need a vision, a plan and someone you trust to act as a sounding board. With that platform, you can do anything. The best part is that it doesn't have to cost you much at all, just time and effort.

I recall a meeting with Alex in his office where we mapped out what I really wanted in life. We put a lot of things on the marker board, including a six-figure income, a successful business that I could sell one day and early retirement. I also stated that I wanted real happiness and contentment in my life. In reality, though, I had three weeks' worth of cash left before I ran out of money.

I needed new business income fast.

Also, the large investment bank, Lehman Brothers had just collapsed. The banking crisis erupted and the world entered into what became a long and deep recession. Coupled with my own personal turmoil, it was not an ideal time to set up a business, but I did it. I had no real choice as state benefits wouldn't cover a fraction of my bills.

I had no marketing budget so I hit the free networking events. I used LinkedIn, set up a simple database from which I could undertake rudimentary mailshots and I contacted anyone that I had met in the past, letting them know what I was up to and what I could offer. I also had someone set up a basic website; I couldn't afford much more.

My previous employer also offered retained consultancy work to me which was a godsend. It gave me a flow of cash that enabled me to rent a small office in Newbury from a good friend, Mia, who ran a successful recruitment business. It felt like a "proper" business having an office to work from, rather than a bedroom.

The office also had the benefit of me mixing and socialising daily with other people. It got me out of the house, the heavy drinking and daytime TV. Mia was also very easy to chat with about business, life and the universe.

I hired my first employee, Kristina. Kristina was another friend and one of my former language students, she came in one day a week to populate the database with new records and information. Kristina was my formative marketing department and also emotional support. It was us against the rest of the world!

So, three people in my life were keeping me anchored, Alex, Mia and Kristina. They cared about me and I drew great strength from that - more than they will ever know. I learned that finding a few, true friends is worth far more than having hundreds of acquaintances.

Some happiness and laughter was starting to creep back into my life. I wasn't quite out of the woods yet. I was still on medication and still drinking too much, but there was some hope, a pinprick of light at the end of the tunnel.

CHAPTER FIVE

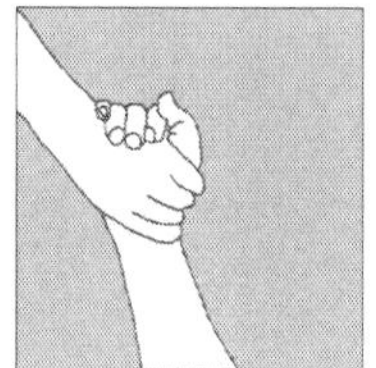

Setbacks

In its first year, my new business made a hundred and ten thousand pounds' turnover. I was delighted! Now, if I could just find a way to grow it into a multi-million pound empire within three years ...

*

The phone rings just as I'm stepping out of the shower. Grasping the towel around me in one hand I gallop to pick it up with the other, dripping freely onto the bedroom carpet.

"Rob!" Roger's voice booms into my ear as always. My largest client and a life-saving retainer, an account worth about three-quarters of my total revenue. Always

worth listening to and keeping happy, especially now that I'm on-track to grow my business fast.

"How are you, Roger? Good to hear from you ..."

"Well, that's just it, old boy. I'm rather afraid we'll have to bring the retainer to an early close. It's this blasted economy – we're just not going to get through the recession without tightening the purse strings, old chap."

My reflection freezes in the mirror in front of me, its eyes looking back into mine. I'm not in my own body right now. I'm in there – in the mirror image of me – not real.

This can't be real.

*

All my plans for future growth faltered. I'd assumed that this client would always loyally be there with me on my journey. I learnt a very harsh lesson in business life: don't get complacent. I hadn't thought of a contingency plan should things not work out the way I hoped.

Now, I was stuck.

My world was rocked for the second time in little over a year. I felt that my short-term success had been cruelly stolen from me – and my flutter of hope in Life along with it.

I wasn't strong enough to weather this. Depression, helplessness and no self-worth came flooding back to haunt me. I spiralled downward once again.

The pain was unbearable. It simply had to be stopped and there was only one way to do that. I decided to stop taking my prescription tablets and to save them up instead. Then, when I had amassed enough, I would take them in one go and bring an end to this painful life. For once, I reasoned, I would be in control of my fortunes, not controlled by external events or other people.

As the depression pressed further on me without the meds, I took alcohol to dull the pain and depression. I ended up keeping those pills for many years; there were over seven hundred of them in the end.

While I waited for the right time to end it all, I came across an advert for a Financial Planning job in Dubai. It was 'commission only' – not the most reliable way to make a living. However, I had been an Independent Financial Adviser in the past; what could be easier than selling financial products to some of the richest people in the world? I had nothing to lose and I could still run my own little UK business remotely from Dubai.

I applied for the job, and, six weeks later, rocked up in the Middle East, eager to start work. I had been promised a database and leads from the company I was working for. I was given neither. What I was given was a twenty-something boss who'd been out there for four years, had the trappings of success and thought he knew everything about selling.

I'm sure he was just as disappointed with me. He'd been given someone twice his age who didn't agree with many of his sales and business techniques.

I suspected it wasn't going to go well in Dubai.

I started to think that I may have jumped from the frying pan into the fire, especially as the temperature in Dubai was over forty-five degrees centigrade in summer.

Still, I had made the decision and so I was determined to make the most of it.

*

To: Kristina, Alex, Mia
*Subject: IS IT SUPPOSED TO BE THIS **** TOUGH ALL THE **** TIME???*
Hi, guys –

Sorry – it's another bollocks message. I'm just feeling so fed up with all the stress over here – well, actually, more than that. To be honest, I'm feeling scared and more than a bit lonely without you guys. Can't you come over for a while? The pressure is just so intense.

I know that I can't on my own. I need you – we're a team. I need my TEAM!!!!!

The problem with a commission only job in a place like Dubai is that your cash runs out pretty quickly if you don't get some early success. It's a 5-star lifestyle but that takes a lot of money to fund it. That's fine if you are employed and receiving £1m+ in salary and paying no tax.

But I'm not!! I'm self-employed and I don't know where the next commission cheque is coming from!! If I can't pay my bills, I might end up in jail. Did you know that??! It's an actual criminal offence in Dubai to owe money!

I'm working round the clock to keep things going here, the little legacy business in the UK and I just can't handle it without you!! You're three thousand miles away.

That's too far. COME OVER!!!!!

Love,

Rob xx

*

My support team felt so very, very far away. I was so lonely on my own, and my loneliness made beautiful, sparkling Dubai seem like a harsh, uncompromising and unforgiving environment. It wasn't, of course; it was the projection of my own state of mind that made it so, but it felt very real to me at the time.

I would wake up most mornings in a panic, having waves of anxiety, then throwing up in the sink. It became a ritual affair before I put on my suit and went to the office in my little hired Toyota. I put a brave face on every day, not wanting others, especially my boss, to be aware of the anguish and turmoil I was in.

This time, it felt worse. Here I was suffering from depression, away from the people closest to me in a foreign country and in a new job, without any certainty of income.

CHAPTER SIX

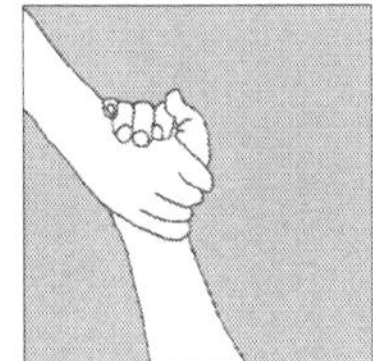

Dubai: brave, new world

Without the promised database of prospects, the flow of leads or a brand, I needed to generate new clients fast. My tiny apartment alone was costing me three thousand pounds per month.

Using LinkedIn, I connected with hundreds of people in Dubai and then started sending out informative articles related to financial planning. I hung out in places my target audience would frequent, such as the Dubai Marina, the Irish Bar, and a whole host of networking groups. I even travelled up and down the country's only arterial motorway, the Sheikh Zayed Road. It is four hundred miles long with six lanes on each carriageway.

Dubai has a plethora of motor dealerships alongside this monstrous motorway: Ferrari, Maserati,

Rolls-Royce, Porsche, and Harley Davidson to name but a few. These were all places my target market would spend their time and money.

It took me two full months to cold call all of the dealerships in Dubai. I offered a free financial planning review as a bolt-on service to automotive customers of those dealerships. Many said "no" but a few said "yes"; one even gave me twelve hundred email addresses of customers they had in the UAE for me to use for my own marketing. Bear in mind that there was no Financial Services Act nor Data Protection legislation, certainly not in Dubai at that time. It was like the "Wild West" out there – everyone for himself, a chance to make big money for those that worked hard and were determined to succeed. My aptitude for single-mindedness was a helpful attribute; I am able to focus completely on something once I've made up my mind to accomplish it.

I can remember one sales call I made was to a partner in a large law firm. He finished the meeting by writing out a personal cheque for three hundred thousand pounds to invest in a product I was offering. Then, he introduced me to his managing partner who ended up writing me another cheque for the same amount. I walked out from their plush offices with six hundred thousand pounds and instantly calculated my commission on those two transactions.

Whoop! Man – I was back on track! I had conquered Dubai!

Or so I thought.

The problem is that those successes aren't every week, but your bills and financial commitments come all too regularly. The immense stress of having to sign people up was overwhelming. I worked round the clock, didn't eat anything apart from chicken and salami, washed down with a lot - and I mean a *lot* - of vodka and tonic.

Dubai is not a "dry" country; if you want alcohol, it's widely available in hotels and restaurants. The Duty-Free shop in the airport is a good start when you first arrive in the country.

Stress, anxiety and being alone all took its toll on me. I started frequenting those suicide websites again and contemplated ending it all in Dubai.

That's when I had my brilliant idea.

Why not go out with a bang? I'd jump off the tallest building in the world, the Burj Khalifa. There'd be no repatriation costs, as there wouldn't have been anything left of me to send back to Britain. Looking at it that way, I could save my family about twenty-five grand.

I also kept a "Death Diary", a journal in which I scribbled down all my thoughts as they came to me. It would be something to leave behind after I had gone to hopefully offer understanding to my family and close friends as to why I had decided to kill myself. It sounds a weird thing to do, but it mattered to me that there was some sort of explanation to my actions. It also turned out to be a useful way of helping to get thoughts racing in my mind onto paper. A kind of therapy, I suppose.

As it happened, that Death Diary was more informative to me than to anybody else. It showed me over a number of months what was important to me and that the impact of my suicide on my four children would be dreadful. They'd probably never forgive me. They constituted the key reason for my keeping going – my not caving to my suicidal thoughts. Looking back, my decision to live came down to the knowledge of the effect that my suicide would have on them. They'd have to live their whole lives knowing that their dad had done such an awful thing and left them behind.

I was torn.

How could I find the strength to dig deeper and hang on for longer? Wouldn't it be so much easier to just give up and let gravity do the work?

That's how I ended up at the top of the Burj Khalifa – where you found me at the start of this book. I had every intention to end my life.

It's eight hundred and thirty metres high, so jumping off it would certainly be final. Had that fire exit door been unlocked as it should have been, you wouldn't be reading this. Who knows whether I would have gone ahead and actually jumped? It's one of those things in life one can never know.

What I do know is that I wasn't given the choice to end my life that day. Circumstances were telling me not to give up – to find another solution.

Thwarted, broken and past caring, I returned to my apartment.

What the hell do I do now? I thought.

CHAPTER SEVEN

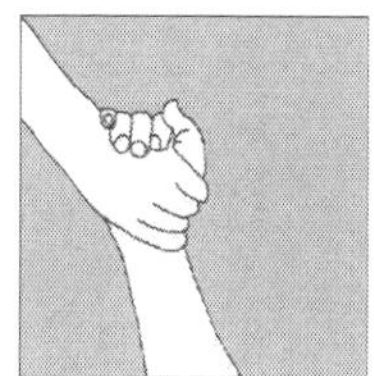

Phone a friend

"There's nothing green in here. All you have is booze and meat."

Alex extricates his head from the depths of my fridge and turns to me with a look of mock despair. "What's going on, mate?"

I can take the teasing. It's just so good that he's here. He leapt on that plane at the words "come and visit me in Dubai - all expenses paid" thank goodness. He's never one to let an offer like that go begging. I'm feeling stronger already for simply having my friend around. These few days are going to be the lifeline I need, I can feel it.

So far, I've mentioned nothing about my abortive suicide attempt. I don't really want to; this is not my finest hour. Besides, he's so busy waxing lyrical about the benefits of having a balanced diet that I doubt I could get a word in. It's just comforting listening to him. Who needs Jiminy Cricket with Alex around?

"Mate, you need to look after yourself better. You can't hope to function properly – even think positively – if you're filling yourself with junk. Here – take this; we'll go and make a grocery list on the roof."

Flipping me a pen and a notepad, Alex picks up two glasses of water with lots of ice and heads for the stairs. He's right: there's really only one place to pontificate Life, the Universe and everything in it and that's at the poolside on top of my apartment, lounging in the sun.

Then, he asks the Big Question:

"Tell me, what is it you want – I mean, really want to do in business life?"

I don't know how he has the knack of asking profound questions but I love it when he does. What do I want? Really, really want ...?

I gaze over the rooftop, over the clear blue pool and into the azure sky beyond. It's peaceful up here; a really good place to relax after a day at work. I don't know why I don't come up here more often. Probably because I never finish working; I'm always stressed out by it. I never seem to get to a point where I can say, "It's done. Time for fun in the sun."

The ice rattles in Alex's glass as he sips, waiting patiently for my response.

I shrug, run my fingers through my hair as my mind automatically shies away from the question.

"I don't know, mate. I really don't know."

He's not put off.

"But if you DID know," he persists, "what would Life look like?"

Boom! What a great follow-up question. He hasn't let me off the hook. Just what if Life could be good? What if there IS a positive future? What if it really could be different to the dismal existence I'm leading right now?

Turning to him, I can't help but smile. The first smile I've genuinely felt for a long, long time. It feels like a pivotal point in my life.

"Well, I'd like to get back to selling businesses for other people. Help them get free by finishing one chapter in their lives and starting a new one."

*

Alex and I had a creative planning session right there on the roof by the pool as to how that might happen. Once more, a little hope glimmered that things might take a turn for the better. You only need to see a speck of light at the end of the tunnel to make your way towards it.

Shortly after he flew back to the UK, I heard from an old friend, Chris Barker. He was on holiday in Dubai and suggested we get together for a beer or three. We hadn't seen each other for twenty-five years when I was "Best Man" at his wedding. We had lost touch over time, but here he was in the Dubai desert, like me.

Meeting him again was excellent. It was as if nothing had changed and we immediately picked up where we had left off. We did some fun things like Go-Kart racing and enjoying the night life of Dubai. I hadn't done anything fun since I'd landed in the country; it had been all work and certainly no play for me so far. Chris changed that.

The third person who helped me survive in the Gulf, albeit unwittingly, was Andrew Prince. Andrew is a highly respected IFA who had spent several years working in Dubai. He was looking to work for the company I was working for and I remember trying to put him off.

"Don't do it, Andrew! Stay where you are, mate."

My experiences hadn't been great but he promptly ignored my advice and joined us the following week.

I was so pleased that he did.

He and I had numerous coffee time chats, lunch in the local Lebanese café and a beer in the evening. We're of a similar age, so it was refreshing to talk with someone on the same level. He also has a dry, sometimes acerbic wit, which I like. He was the voice of reason in a mad environment. We became good friends and remained so for years after.

Without thinking, I had built my small support network in the UAE, just like I had done in the UK.

You only need one or two good friends to help you cope with life. It's not the multitude that will help, it's a few special people that happen to come into your life at the right time. The multitude tends to ignore you when you need it.

Even though things were improving, it became clear that the UK was calling me home. So over Ramadan I wrote to twenty accountancy firms, saying that I was "an experienced corporate financier currently in the Middle East and looking to return back to the UK. Do you have a role for me?"

Surprisingly, five firms responded positively and I flew back to the UK for interviews. The one I eventually decided to go with wasn't an employed position; rather, it was a new business set up with me taking the roles of shareholder and Managing Director. Everyone in the business put money in but I was the only one working in it. Altogether, we had fourteen investors on board and a real vision for the future.

Evolution Complete Business Sales Ltd was born.

CHAPTER EIGHT

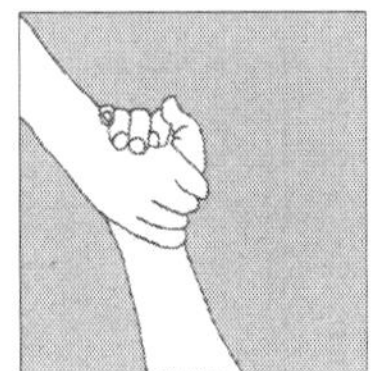

Confidence

Setting up in business is never easy. Setting up during a recession is even less so.

However, the support and encouragement from my fellow investors was extremely valuable. For once, I didn't feel alone in business. I had other people around me with convergent interests.

My previous experiences of working as a 'one-man band' and then working without a salary in a foreign country stood me in good stead: I had unwittingly developed skills – of survival, resourcefulness and creativity – that I would never have discovered had I remained in banking. I truly felt that the last few years had been an apprenticeship for something more substantive in my business life. My past "failures" would equip me for the future but for now I was battling a few old demons.

*

I'm a total fraud.

Here I am, sitting in the car and about to go into a meeting with some of the top earners in the country. All I have to show for myself is a new business with no track record and my ever-present depression.

The familiar wave of nausea and surge of adrenaline washes over me as I contemplate what has to happen in my next hour's pitch.

At least I can pretend to be confident. It's all in the energy – stride energetically into the room, keep your head up ... I tilt my chin up and practice my most lifelike smile. I can show enthusiasm. Normally, when I'm chatting with a client, I genuinely am interested in his situation and what he needs. As soon as I feel engaged like that, I feel my old energy resurge.

Still, that's not going to be enough in the long term. Businesspeople of this ilk can sniff out timidity at two hundred yards. What's that expression? "If you want to play with the big dogs, learn to pee in the tall grass."

I'm already playing with the big dogs. I fear I'm about to get mauled. I check my teeth in the rear view mirror, straighten my shoulders and wish my reflection good luck.

It's a pity self-confidence isn't something you can buy.

Or is it?

*

While it's true that you can pretend to be confident and project confidence, many see through it. I would go into panic mode routinely before a sales pitch or a presentation for an event.

It was time to get some help. I sat at the computer and did a good search for somebody who might be able to help me in this area.

"Tracey Miller – Confidence Coach" popped up on my screen before long. I'd never heard of a 'confidence coach' but it sounded as though one was exactly what I needed.

Tracey was fabulous. She let me talk and talk, just asking me pertinent questions from time to time. She helped me to face my deep fears in life over a period of just a few months. She also tapped into my long-term life goal of being on a Greek island, teaching English when I hit fifty-five years old.

She helped me see that it wasn't just dealing with the issues of today; it was about setting my sights on the future and having wonderful and exciting goals and ambitions to achieve in life.

One key aspect I've discovered is that it's okay to be yourself. People like authenticity and naturalness, they respond positively to it. Being human is a natural state to be in. For too many years I had tried to pretend to be someone I wasn't.

Being myself, warts 'n all, creates a good state of mind. I found that I enjoyed "being in the moment". In other words, my recognising and enjoying the things around me rather than striving and dashing from one thing to another, without truly experiencing them.

Tracey and her partner, George Swift, are two of the most inspiring people I have met. I have been part of their BBB Success Group and more latterly their Mastermind Group in Berkshire. They run forums for like-minded business owners to share their business problems and their successes in a supportive and positive environment.

It can be lonely at the top, so it's really important to link up with other peers.

CHAPTER NINE

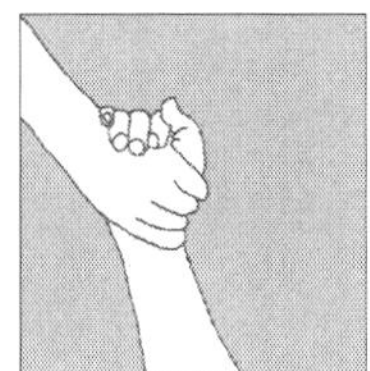

Onwards and upwards

So, there I was, in early 2011, with a new business called Evolution. Even its name was a reflection of my own life journey. You'd have thought that I'd been put off running a business by now but it was different this time.

This time, I had some working capital from investors so I could pay myself a salary from Day One. I had time to do the right things in the right order. Planning and preparation could be done properly.

Do you know that more than one in three business start-ups never see their third anniversary? A common failing is the lack of proper planning and market research. Too many business owners just jump in and start burning cash on initiatives and things that turn out to be mistakes. Unless you have deep pockets and love this 'fly by the seat of your pants' approach, a more considered and planned approach is far preferable.

Here's a checklist of questions to address in a business plan;

1. What exactly are you offering to the market?
2. What problem does it solve?
3. Why would someone buy it?
4. Who else offers something similar?
5. Why should someone choose to buy from you, rather than elsewhere?

Create a realistic and prudent 3-year growth plan of anticipated sales and related costs.

Make sure too that you have sufficient working capital. Whatever you believe you need, add another 50%.

What is your "plan B" if it goes wrong?

My goal was to create a £million business within five years. I also wanted to return to my long-term goal of retiring at the age of fifty-five and to teach English from a Greek island.

There is something healthy about having a longer-term plan for your life rather than just making money from growing a business. Money is purely a short-term motivator; it does not satisfy in the long term.

I've experienced this in my own life. I've been rich and I've been poor at different points in my life, several times. Possessions count for very little in reality; it's a significance and purpose in life that matter far more. It's all about your having a reason to get up on a Monday morning with an excitement for the week; a sense that what you're doing matters to someone or something.

So, I had a vision, a plan and financial backing: now, I had to make it happen.

I believed that I could make it happen since I had been through the mill in setting up two micro businesses previously, one in 2008 and the other in 2010 in Dubai. I had learnt skills and tactics that would help me in growing Evolution CBS and had seven years' experience of selling businesses for another brokerage.

Added to that, with Tracey's help, I now had confidence that, with my expertise built up in the industry, EvolutionCBS would be successful.

Self-confidence is a key attribute for many successful business owners. You need to believe that you are right and that success will follow.

The other quality that should follow is the ability to listen to the wise counsel of others. In my experience, this is often harder for business owners to embrace, particularly if they have encountered some success. Why should they listen to the advice of others if what they are doing is already working well?

This thinking can be a pitfall since the success may not have been down to the business owner. Perhaps he or she just got lucky – been at the right place at the right time. What's more, who's to say how much more success might have followed had other people been asked for their input, support and ideas?

It's something I still tussle with. My starting point in my head is that I know what needs to be done to make something work and it's down to others to show or prove to me that there is a better way. It's not an ideal mindset I would admit; I'm a work in progress on that front.

CHAPTER TEN

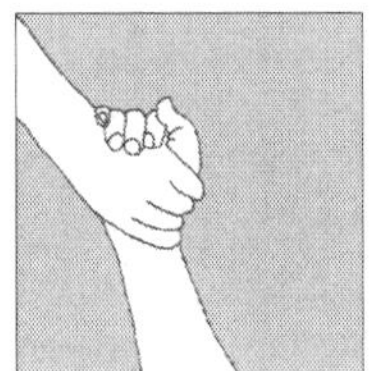

How to create success

Hopefully, you have not just turned to this chapter without reading the preceding chapters. If you have, go back to the beginning as it will mean more and provide context.

Go on! Stop jumping ahead ...

You see, there are no get rich quick plans that work. It's grit, determination, previous failures, serendipity and a little bit of luck that creates a successful business.

The blueprint for the growth of EvolutionCBS came from reading "The Beermat Entrepreneur" by Mike Southon and Chris Weet (Pearson Education Ltd, 2015). According to the authors, I needed to establish four pillars to the business, with myself at the centre. Those four pillars would in time become the Senior Team that would run the business day-to-day and help to release me as the owner. Effectively, I would be 'on' the business rather than 'in' it, as Michael Gerber would say. His book, "The E-Myth Revisited" (Harper Collins, 2001) is another inspirational book for me.

I wanted to start with the initial pillar of 'Marketing'. You can be a fantastic salesperson but if you don't have a good flow of qualified leads you're sunk.

My first hire was Kay. She came highly recommended to me by our mutual friend, Mia, so no recruitment fee! What appealed to me about Kay was that she was an accomplished marketing person with extensive commercial experience. She'd also run her own business successfully for seven years which was a great bonus for me.

She's proven to be a first-class hire: highly professional, knowledgeable, flexible and a real grafter. For a while, it was just Kay and me working together. She would create visibility for the business, generating leads and I would follow them up and start to secure new, retained clients.

After a number of months, it became clear that I needed a second pillar – that of 'Operations'. I couldn't sell and then at the same time undertake delivery of the service. For that, I engaged two people, James and Claire. Both of them had worked for me before in the same industry, so I had first-hand experience of their strengths and weaknesses. They were both available at the right time, so again I had no recruitment fees at all.

The third pillar of the business, 'Finance', was provided by my investors as they were accountants.

I have learnt so much over the years from them about financial reporting and interpreting figures. To know your numbers gives you comfort and you can sleep at night. I meet too many fellow business owners that do not have a clue how much money their business is making. They don't budget for the year and they don't review the financial performance monthly. I want to sleep at night knowing there is a sufficient cash buffer in the bank (say, three months' worth) and that there will be no unwelcome surprises with unexpected bills surfacing.

If an owner says "I'm not an accountant" my response is always that you don't need to be. You just need to be on top of your own numbers as part of being a competent director. Remember, you can make a loss a number of times but you can only run out of cash once!

The fourth pillar was 'Sales' – but I took myself out of the running. To fill that position, I turned to my old boss from my banking days, Steve. He was a person I looked to for sales coaching and inspiration. He's the commensurate deal closer and when he became available, I approached him. No recruitment agency involved again.

Engaging someone to take on the new business development side from me was critical. A business that's reliant on the owner's skills and involvement is worth far less than one that isn't. As an owner, it's imperative that you bring into the business people who are better at their roles than you are. Effectively, you need to make yourself redundant from your own businesses.

Business acquirers avoid purchasing owner-reliant businesses. If they ever do invest in one, it's at a heavily discounted price. To them, it's like buying a car without an engine.

Also, don't think that, as the outgoing owner, you can stay on for a couple of years under new ownership. It rarely works. After all, when was the last time you had a boss? Can you imagine someone telling you 'no' and to do as you're told?

I didn't think so.

EvolutionCBS is a four-pillar business now, just as described in "The Beermat Entrepreneur". We've also employed others along the way, each with specific skills and something valuable to add to the growing team. Rarely have I had to pay a recruitment agency fee ... I'll bet you are spotting a trend here!

*

The hardest transition I've found in growing a business is letting go of its day to day running. When you have cash invested, plus blood, sweat and tears, it's not easy at all to let others in the team run the business. Many business owners feel that no-one can run their business as well as they do. That may be true in some cases but without delegation and empowerment of key staff, the business will surely plateau in performance. It always does.

This is because there are only seven days in the week - even for we business owners.

That is why I made the hardest decision in business so far. I replaced myself at the centre with someone better than I as Managing Director: the missing piece of the jigsaw, Mike Whittle. I passed the reins of the business over to him for the day-to-day running of my company ... my own company that I gave birth to all those years ago, now in someone else's hands.

It was an immense moment of letting go of something to which I had a huge emotional attachment. But it was essential were the business to continue on its growth trajectory. Mike and I had worked together in my banking days and, in the intervening years, had run a number of much larger businesses than Evolution. He was a trusted person and, as importantly, he'd worked successfully in the larger, private business arena – a space to which I'd envisaged Evolution transitioning.

The secret to growing a successful business is to find the right people, trust them and supply sufficient resources to help them achieve their goals and targets, both personal and business ones.

*

As owners, we're there primarily to set direction, monitor results and make the big decisions within the business. It's tempting to interfere but resist it at all costs.

The business has grown and flourished. I eventually bought out my original seed investors. There is a season for everything and the time had come to part company. It's not uncommon to have divergent interests at Board level; it's very normal in fact. The business was valued at £1.5m at that time - not bad from a cold start, during a recession and within just five years or so.

Subsequently, I brought in three new investors - all three of them highly successful entrepreneurs in their own right. Each of them has something fresh to bring to the table for the next phase in Evolution's growth cycle.

The last few pages have been the mechanics behind how I grew my business from scratch and into something sustainable, profitable and scalable.

The other key element is my inner drive and determination to win through. A "whatever it takes" mentality to ensure that success prevails. I've often been accused of being stubborn. Well, I think it's an asset when starting and growing your own business. It's a huge advantage to have a complete conviction that what you're doing is right and will succeed over a period of time.

I have always had real "intent" behind any of my life plans. Yes, some doubt has come in over the years, but it doesn't last long as it's overcome by energy, passion and a will to win. Perhaps it's innate. I'm not entirely sure, but I really don't like to lose at anything. Certainly, quitting a project goes against the grain for me.

Stubbornness can be a virtue. I cherish my ability to dig my heels in and remain adamant about something. Clearly, it's a two-edged sword and there are other qualities that are important in Life ... When it comes to running a business, though, I believe a clear and dogged determination to succeed is a great starting point.

CHAPTER ELEVEN

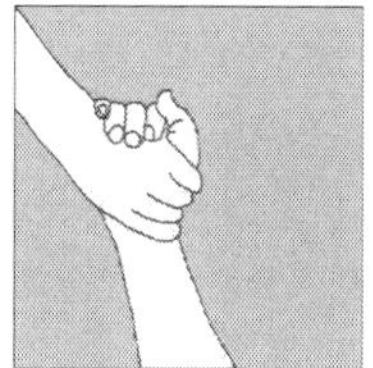

What's next for me?

I love being involved with EvolutionCBS, but I don't need to run it day in and day out. My Senior Team can do that far better than I, led by Mike.

It's taken years to recruit the right team to run the business day to day on my behalf. When you start a one-man band business you need to do everything. As you grow, there's the need to bring in others to share some of the workload. The knack of 'being on the business, not in it' has been my finding and attracting people better than I in the wide variety of roles in the business. I've made myself redundant from the very business I started all those years ago – and it feels wonderful!

Letting go of control is hard for most business owners. Many derive a sense of significance and purpose in making most of the day to day decisions. To willingly give that up is extremely difficult for most and for some proves impossible.

It has taken years for me to relinquish the day to day control. It didn't come naturally to me. But I knew it was essential were I ever to move on to fulfil my long-term vision of teaching English from a double decker bus around the Mediterranean, with the woman of my dreams, by 2020.

However, I have "retired" - and a year earlier than the deadline I set for myself. Retirement to me is about my being able to do the things I want to do, when I want to do them and with the people that I want to be with.

So, in 2019, I devised my 10-year plan to create a "living legacy" in my life. It will take me to the age of 65, so I affectionately refer to it as my OAP plan ("Old Age Pensioner" plan). Building a living legacy centres around giving back in life and to make a difference in other people's lives. A charitable foundation to house a diverse range of altruistic activities and investments to help others that are in need and struggling in life. Along with long term friend and now partner in life, Kristina, we will build something that will touch other people's lives in a variety of ways.

I want to help people who are suffering from depression, particularly men. Eight hundred thousand people every year take their own lives and of that number 75% are men!

We men seem to be far more susceptible to this global crisis. Maybe we are more inclined to keep quiet when times are really tough. We put on a brave face and try to carry on, carrying an ever-growing weight.

I have first-hand experience in that. It's my mission to start a conversation with men around the world. A conversation about how they feel when their life collapses and, just as importantly, how they fight back and provide themselves hope for the future.

My partner, Kristina, has a real heart and passion to set up a children's orphanage in her home country of Albania. Health care and provision of the country's more vulnerable is patchy at best. There's very limited support and care for those most exposed to some of Life's harshness. She wants to make a real difference in the lives of children. One possibility for us is to provide free English additional lessons to Albanian children, from that double decker bus. Education is key for people - especially younger children - to change their future. Improving their English skills will help to open up a whole new world, maybe beyond the borders of Albania. There's a whole new world awaiting them in further education and employment on an international basis.

All of this charitable work requires funding, of course. The plan is to develop several income streams. I read once that the average multi-millionaire has eight sources of income. I aim to at least double the capital that I've built up in the last ten years, triple my current income but then to give much of it away via a charitable foundation. My parents always taught me that it's better to give than receive; it's been only in later life that I have discovered that to be true.

There is infinitely more pleasure in giving to someone than storing money up for materialistic purposes. You can't take it with you when you die, so why not use money for good and to make a difference to others? Better to build a legacy when you are alive, so that you can experience the difference it makes to others rather than to leave it after you've died in a will.

Money is a tool, not an end in itself. I had to learn that the hard way. It nearly ended my life.

Another key aspect to the next ten years is to develop my own private business, focused on three areas: investing my own money into small business ventures, public speaking and mentoring. In all three I have many years' experience; more importantly, though, these are things that I love doing in life. There's nothing more miserable than doing a job that you hate, wishing you were somewhere else.

To that end, I invested in a business earlier this year called "The Kingmaker Group". It primarily helps people bored and frustrated with corporate life to start their own businesses with someone else's money. What they need to bring to the table is energy, commitment and sweat to make it work. I love this concept of changing your life for the better and it goes to the heart of my belief system. You can have anything in life; you just can't have *everything*.

Changing your life, especially when you are battling depression, takes immense courage. It also usually requires the help of other people. Several key people came along for me at just the right time; some might even call them 'angels'.

When I returned to the UK from Dubai in 2011, Tracey helped me with my confidence to make my long-term vision specific and timebound. I have been a committed member of her and her partner's 'Success and Mastermind' groups ever since. My accountability to and responsibility for other positive, fellow business owners has been an important element in my business success – not to mention my personal development. I've learnt so much from other people and, critically, have felt tremendously supported.

Kristina has been a good friend throughout. She's known me wealthy and poor, but our friendship has never changed. When you have money, you have lots of 'friends'. When you lose that money, though, you really find out who your true friends are. Now, we are partners in life together. She is a real grounding influence in my life. Someone who speaks her mind and possesses an uncanny habit of seeing things with pragmatism and a common-sense approach. She makes things simple in life and I love that about her. As humans, we often over-complicate life, when really it's much simpler than we think. Remembering this helps to dilute worry, anxiety and stress.

Lastly, there's Alex. Without his being there to talk to in Dubai and to help me get my life back in perspective, I probably wouldn't be here now. He flew a seven thousand-mile round trip for us to talk in 2010 – to have a proper conversation about Life and the future. He made time to listen and, thank God, he did.

You see, most depressed people just want someone to listen to them and without judgement. They don't want to be a burden, but at the same time, do want to articulate how they are feeling. The old adage "a problem shared, is a problem halved" is true. Somehow, the act of expressing your feelings to another person is essential. Suicide doesn't kill; it's isolation that kills.

If you're feeling on the edge right now and that your life is devoid of hope, find an 'Alex'. Someone you trust with whom you can start a conversation. However, if Life is okay for you right now, be an 'Alex' to someone else. Pick up on the clues that someone you know is really struggling with life. Give them some of your time, really listen and don't offer to fix everything. Just making time and being there for a coffee, a chat, perhaps lunch somewhere on a regular basis is perhaps all they need to stabilise their life.

Time is one thing that we can't buy but we can give it freely to others. It's probably the most precious gift we all possess.

EPILOGUE

During my time of recovery from depression I had to face my demons. By that, I mean that I needed to fix a few things that were left over from my time in stunning Dubai. I left the UAE a defeated man; I felt I had failed. Yes, I had a hope for re-building my life in the UK but there was still something nagging inside me that told me that I needed to go back someday and make a success of things there. Otherwise, I knew it would be something in my life that was dark and oppressive. It was unfinished business.

So, in 2016, my UK Mergers and Acquisitions company's first overseas office was set up in Dubai. Although I went through hell and back during my time over there in 2010, it was to do with me, not the country itself. Dubai is a fantastic country, brimming with opportunity for those who work hard. Despite my weak mental state, I learnt some key skills such as generating new business without data, marketing collateral or back office support. I also had an appreciation of the business culture and things that make the UAE unique. This all helped me set up a new M&A business in the pulsating heart of the Dubai financial district.

Initially, it was just me on my own, flying in every couple of months, making contacts, speaking at events and generating a few clients. It started to work well and there was clearly a market for us, so my trips became more frequent. Eventually, I made the decision to set up a fully-fledged, limited company there with Emirati sponsors. Going into business with Arabs was not something I would ever have thought possible back in 2010. Now, we are in business together and it's a totally enriching experience. We are a formally registered company in the UAE with a trade licence, premises and staff. I've also taken the opportunity to fly over many of my UK staff and Associates for 'working holidays'. Their being exposed to a different culture and ways of doing things is enriching for them, too.

The business is Dubai was profitable from day 1 and continues to be so. I've appointed a director to run it and so I have come full circle again, this time with an overseas business: starting up, nurturing and then creating a success plan for it to be run without my day to day involvement.

*

The overhead light comes on with a soft "bong", reminding us to fasten our seat belts.

Around me, people finish putting away their laptops and tablets, stow their bags in the compartments above and carefully fold their suit jackets in their laps as they sit down. There's something hypnotic about the constant hum of the engines, especially as the plane starts its descent.

I feel a familiar pressure inside my head and turn to look through the window with a smile. Dubai stretches beneath us, glittering and beckoning in the sunshine. In a few minutes' time, I'll be walking through the outside doors of the terminal to be hit suddenly and exhilaratingly by the heat and humidity before meeting my friend at Arrivals. That's what I call a warm welcome. Dubai is a special place for me that's full of hope and opportunity.

As I gaze on the sparkling city below me from such a height, I think back for a moment on how I've looked Failure in the face and defeated it.

Inside, my outlook today is completely different.

It is me who has changed – not my surroundings.

Everyone needs an 'Alex' in their life

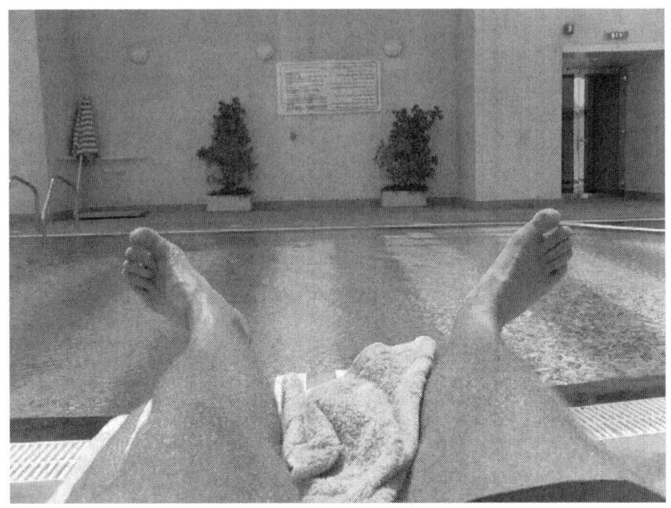

The moment my new business was devised

I conquered my demons, no longer a beaten man

ACKNOWLEDGMENTS

A special mention to Alex Petty and Tracey Miller, both of whom were fundamental in my path of recovery. You are both very special and were the right people at the right time for me. In a very busy world, to have people that take time to really listen and genuinely care is precious.

Also, thanks to my editor on this book, Jo Collie, who has helped me turn my rambling thoughts and personal experiences into something that I believe is clear, concise and compelling, in order to help others struggling with life.

Finally, Dr Andrea Pennington, without whom I may never have had the confidence to share my very personal story with the wider world.

CONTACT THE AUTHOR

Connect with me, I'd love to hear from you...

www.linkedin.com/in/robgoddard

rob.goddard@robgoddard.co.uk

www.robgoddard.co.uk

LEAVE A MESSAGE

In the spirit of our mission to help as many men as possible who are suffering from depression and anxiety, there are some blank pages here where you can add your own thoughts and messages. Your words of encouragement will be read by future readers every time this book is passed on to someone else who needs it. Thank you for your contribution.